God's Country and My People

GOD'S COUNTRY AND MY PEOPLE

by Wright Morris

University of Nebraska Press

Lincoln and London

First Bison Book printing: 1981

Most recent printing indicated by first digit below:

1   2   3   4   5   6   7   8   9   10

Library of Congress Cataloging in Publication Data

Morris, Wright, 1910–
   God's country and my people.

   1. United States—Social life and customs—1945–1970—
Pictorial works. 2. United States—Description and travel—
1960–   —Views. I. Title.
E169.02.M65 1981   973.9   80–23155
ISBN 0–8032–3067–2 (pbk.)

Published by arrangement with the author

Acknowledgment is due to Harcourt, Brace & World, Inc.,
for use of first page from *Babbitt* by Sinclair Lewis.
Copyright 1922 by Harcourt, Brace & World, Inc.

Let me try and explain. From things about to disappear I turn away in time. To watch them out of sight, no, I can't do it.

SAMUEL BECKETT

Is it a house or an ark? A scud seems to blow on the sea of grass and the land falls away like the sea from a swell. On the receding horizon waves of plain break like a surf. The colors run where the grain stirs, or bleed where the blacktop smokes like an oil slick, or evaporate into a shimmering blur of heat and light. The color scheme is sun-dried denim and kiln-dried earth. Like the sea there is no shade. There is no place to hide. A mindless wind fills the void, but nobody hears it: it's the thunderclap of silence that wakes the sleeper. The mast of a dead tree, its spar shattered, tilts to the leeward its tattered rigging; in the winter it is locked in a sea of dry ice. The man who built the house had a whaleman's eyes in a plainsman's face. He brought the clapboards in by ox cart over the rolling cattle trail up from Salinas. A windy crossing. Little wonder this house resembles an ark. The porch is gone from the front, shingles from the roof, and the last tenants went thataway with the Okies—except for those who stand, immaterial, at the windows, or move about with the creak of hinges. The land has tired of the house but it will not soon be free of the inhabitants.

PILLARS of cloud loom on the horizon and at night there is lightning and claps of thunder: from one window or another rain can be seen falling somewhere—usually somewhere else. The blaze of noon frosts the glass. Everywhere the tongue is dry but the mind is wet. Towns spring up like weeds where it rains, dry up when it stops. In the heat of the day the plain itself seems to dissolve into the sky, and a town takes on, like a sunning lizard, the colors of the plain. The lone tree, a dead cottonwood, can be seen by the shadow it casts to the east, a hole prepared for the tree's burial. Indians, according to the record, asked permission to bury their dead in the branches, and while the body was there the barren limbs had been black with crows. The men called it God's country—but the women asked, who else wants it? That's how it happened, the origin of a species, the corn bowls, the cotton bowls and the dust bowls. The tall corn flowers and burns in the wind but the plain remains a metaphysical landscape, the bumper crop a harvest of weather, fiction and romance.

Some time before this landscape became a state, it was a state of mind. The land itself was tipped so the waters flowed eastward, and where they flowed underground they called it Nebraska. There were few records. There was no history. Time was reckoned according to the plagues and blizzards. The territory itself was not yet part of the Union and only the hand of God had shaped it. That was what the Grandfather found pleasing, if not his bride. They crossed the wide Missouri on a ferry and traveled west, by wagon, along the Platte Valley. Antelope were seen. Wolves were reported. Beyond the dry river rose the coasts of Nebraska, a scud blowing on the sea of wind-whipped grass. Its color varied where the buffalo had been slaughtered, the hides stacked. Under the grass she remarked the wheel tracks of the wagons, the mounds of looted graves. Flowers without names grew along the wayside; between the leaves of her Bible she pressed those that bloomed only at night. The Grandfather had an eye for other details. Many things would come to pass, but the nature of the place would remain a matter of opinion—a log drying in the sun or the dry bed of a river seen from space.

THE Grandfather built the house in such haste he forgot about the stairs between the upstairs and the downstairs. A hole had to be sawed in the floor, with a ladder inserted as in a hayloft. Climbing up and down it his wife grew weak, his children grew strong. The bedroom featured a window with panes of church glass that made a pattern of color on the bedclothes. In the evening sunset the window burned like a house on fire. The Grandmother, bedridden with childbirth, had an eye for such details. As if she feared what she might see in her sleep, she often slept with her eyes open. The moon seemed to emerge, like a swollen pumpkin, from the shingled roof of the privy; between the house and the barn the yard was like a table scoured by the wind. Invisible as air, it nevertheless made itself seen. Against the crack of dawn, like light beneath a door, the Grandmother watched the foolish chickens leave the hen house, then sail off, like paper bags, in a puff of the wind. Some were caught in the mesh of chicken-wire fence, others disappeared. The wind-honed yard gave them no hold, and even the cats crossed the yard on their bellies, as if stalking birds. The Grandmother saw plainly that all visible things were made or unmade by invisible forces, impersonal, impartial, and inexhaustible as the prevailing wind.

THE spider spun its web, the hawk circled on the sky, the ring around the moon prophesied the weather, and the names of the children, like pressed flowers, filled the flyleaf of the family Bible: Dwight and Winona, Myron and Violet, Marion and Grace. In the portrait taken at the turn of the century the eldest son, Dwight, resembles fearless, steely-eyed William S. Hart. All eyes, but two, are tilted upward at the birdie and the grace God sheds on the country. Those of my mother stare level into the camera as if to see the culprit hiding behind it. That would be my father. The future on which she fastened her gaze would prove to be me. I have lived into the world she was denied, but who can say her eyes are not still on it? It is known that I have them, and the look they give you is said to be hers.

On my mother's side I am descended from God and a mingling of the races at the Battle of Hastings. I have it from my Aunt Winona, an authority. God and man, working in close collaboration, first settled and then improved God's country, where responsibilities and rewards were equally shared. In the name of God and westward course of empire the Grandfather settled the coasts of Nebraska; the line of descent, from God to man, is easily traced. On the Lord's day, from dawn to dusk, the Grandfather did His will and observed His customs—which left him six long days and nights to work for himself. He served both masters well. He left his stamp on the land, his mark on his neighbors, his will on his issue unto the fourth generation, and features known to be his still quarrel for my face. It is with his stubborn assurance that I both measure his folly and respect his faith.

At EIGHTY-SIX, when I first set eyes on him, he stood erect, apple-cheeked and cheerful, hitched to the plow with which he had personally broken the plains. The shifting line between himself and the horse had disappeared. He wore the harness. He stood there with the sagging reins in his hands. It was well known that he drove everything he put these hands on—loved ones and feared ones, good ones and bad ones—so why, when the time came, shouldn't he drive himself? He made this country what it is, and what it is makes this country hard to remake.

OVERHEAD the sons of pioneers jet to appointments in Miami, Dallas and New York, the receding horizon bounded by the curves of the airline hostess. Here below, and best seen from above, the westward trek of empire merges with the prairie, the lines once worn into the landscape are wearing out. In the blowouts on the rise, raked clean of arrowheads, are the potsherds of the new conquerors: hubcaps, beer cans, old tires, bedsprings and green bottle glass. The buffalo have been slaughtered, the ghosts have departed, the red skin and the black skin retired to reservations, and a man accustomed to the ruins of war would feel right at home. It is all there to be seen until the tidal shift of sand conceals one disaster in order to reveal another. One cannot escape it. There is nothing to see but parallels. The plow that broke the plains lies buried in the yard, and it is clear that the plains won the return engagement. And that is the story: a skirmish won, a battle lost.

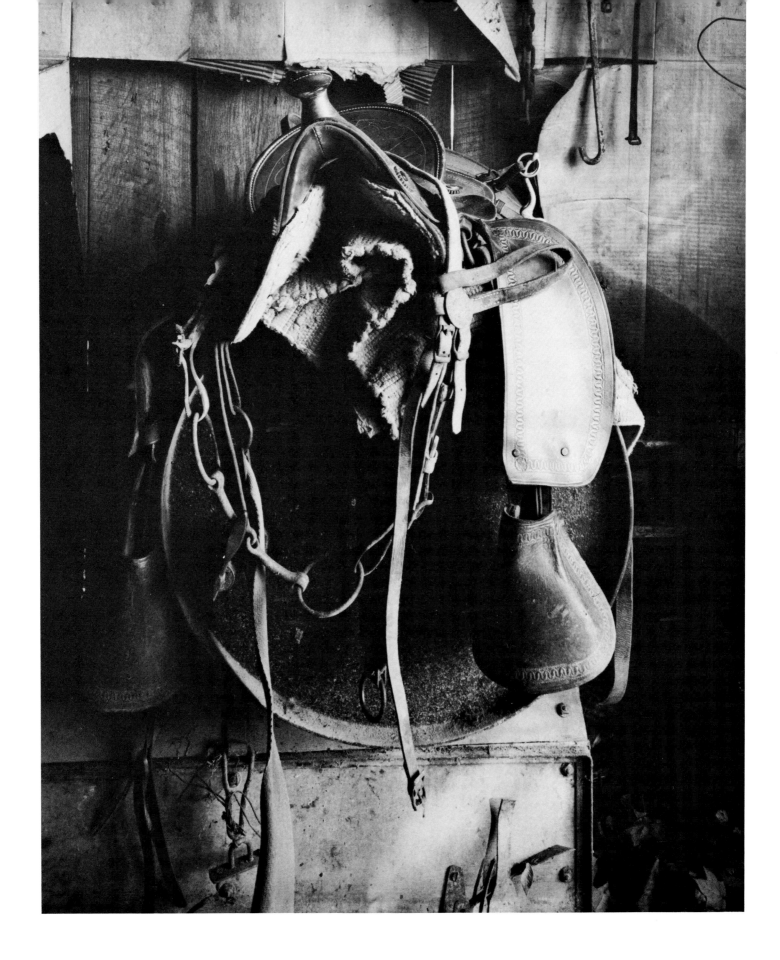

A MACHINE for contemplation, a throne for reflection, a couch for taking in or giving out information, capable of elevation, bodily suspension, facial and tonsorial transformation, the iron age went on to more imposing constructions but none of them so well scaled to the nature of man. Seated on a cushioned board placed across the chair arms, I first appraised the world from a point of elevation, observed my new head emerge from the old one, experienced the baptism of the green tonic water, held my breath in the cloud of fragrant talcum, and as I descended heard the voice of authority pronounce the code word "Next." In the mirror where the things of this world were reflected my father and mother exchanged their first glances, an Eden full of the ringing chirp of Cahow's shears. Over the half-curtain at the front window my father observed my mother descending from a buggy. The barber cloth dangling from his neck like a napkin, he had leaped from the chair to help her. That's the story, and who am I to contradict it? It has the smell of fact and the ring of good fiction. Further facts are that I have the hair of one on the other's head. Eddie Cahow, his shears quiet, remarked on that fact more than thirty years later. "It's your mother's hair," he said, snipping himself a sample, "but takes the clippers at the back like your daddy. You like it wet or dry?"

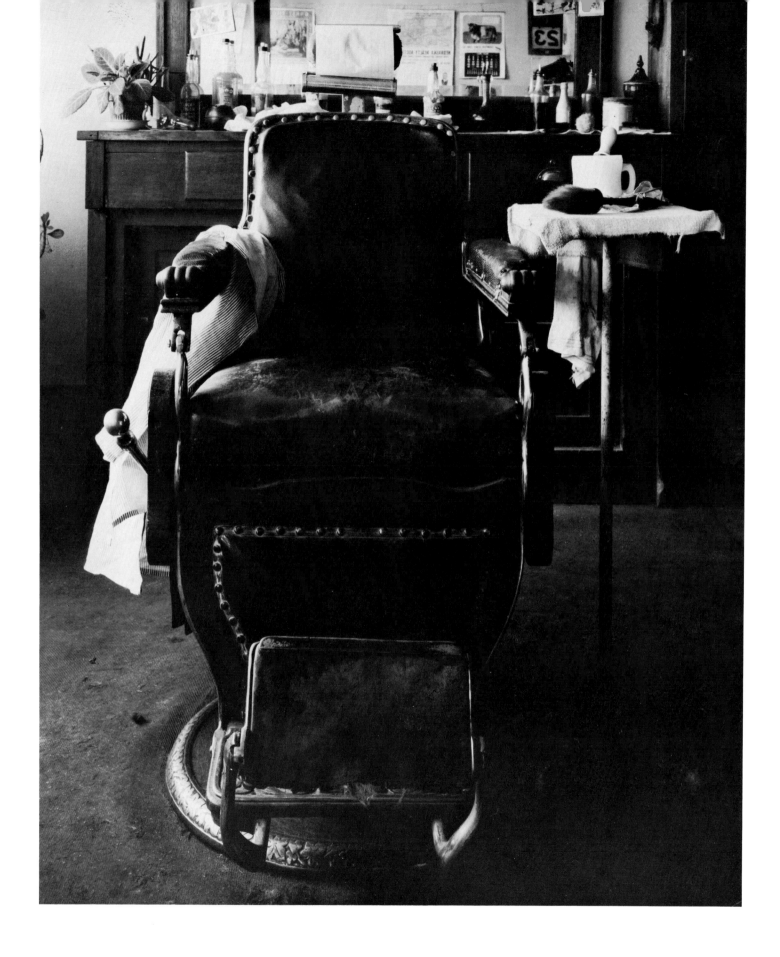

IN THIS metaphysical landscape my mother lived an existential life. "You see off there—" my uncle said, as if he saw her, and wagged his finger at the insulators on a power pole. Two were gone. He cocked his thumb and fired as if to shoot off another. "Why, boy, you should have seen her. A crack shot with a rifle. She could crack them like eggs from the seat of the buggy. Why, boy—" he repeated, but there words failed. I tried to see her, as he did, on the lids of my eyes. I had not thought of my mother as another Annie Oakley. Knowing my father, I knew that he looked for other talents from a woman in the seat of a buggy.

I said, "What would she shoot at today?"

"At the moon," he said, matter-of-factly, and squinted at the jet streams on high heaven. Time had not dimmed her image. "She liked the newest and best. She wanted to live right here and now."

Here and now, his brown hand slapped his knee and set his foot to wagging. He wore box-toe, hook-and-eye shoes over mixed-blue work socks he bought in bound packs of a dozen, saving the twine. My mother had a short life with my father but a long one with those who loved her, whose assignment has been to relate the then and there to the here and now.

Eddie Cahow came up from Texas on the Chisholm Trail, headed for the green grass of Wyoming, a genuine blue-glaze razor and a double swing strop in his pack. He stopped off to give the ailing local barber a hand. When this man died, he naturally stayed on till he found a man to take his place. That took time. The westbound trains out of Omaha no longer stopped. He married a local girl, built her a house with a porch, put a furnace in the basement, planted a tree to shade the lawn swing, added plants and a gum ball machine to the barbershop. One chair proved to be enough. Cranked up in the chair he could see over the half-curtain at the window. Natives who took off for other places sent him postcards he tucked into the mirror. One was from my father and mother on their honeymoon. The view was that of San Francisco and the Golden Gate. He wrote to say having wonderful time, and asked Cahow to wire him fifty dollars. Cahow wired it back: in a man's life he went on just one honeymoon. My father wrote the card with an indelible pencil which he moistened at his lips before making periods. These he drilled through the card, then smeared with the heel of his hand. He was good at postcards since they required less than ten words, like a good wire. *Have gun, will travel* would have impressed my father as a sensible message, a little on the cryptic side. He semaphored greetings, wrote a prose style fashioned by the Morse code.

THE Grandfather's first-born married a girl from Kansas and was next heard from on the Texas Panhandle. They planted winter wheat on a section of virgin land fenced in by rows of white-faced cattle. The tractor never stopped coughing. When he brought it in after plowing all night, his wife drove it off. The dust that trailed out behind screened off the cattle and the rabbits that hopped out of the reach of the gang plows. It was on the eggs they ate in the morning and powdered the sills in Wichita and Kansas City. It caked the roots of his teeth, pitted westbound windshields, and sanded the hills of Nebraska with Texas. Topsoil yellowed the sky over Chicago and thickened the delta in Louisiana; the landscape could be seen flowing beneath the bridges, moiling rivers of earth. The land was on the march ahead of the people, a new pioneer twist. With a kerosene tractor, his wife and a dream my Uncle Dwight invented the dust bowl, helped change the course of empire and, thanks to the prevailing wind, brought the grit of God's country to the sidewalks of New York.

WHILE his wife handled the tractor Dwight would sit on the gang-plows letting his hand drag in the loam of the furrow. He liked that. He left the dirt caked under his nails. He could walk a quarter-mile with two gas-filled milk cans or calculate sums without pencil and paper, his fingers pressed to his eyelids, his steel-rimmed glasses pushed back on his head. A fine powder of dust, like talcum, kept his body soft and dry in the winter: in the spring he would wipe it off with a towel before he took his bath. The year he had a crop he bought a Willys Knight sedan and took his wife to the Carlsbad Caverns. In one cavern stood a column sixty million years old, built up drop by drop by the drip from the ceiling. In the presence of this column he felt both inspired and stupefied. To understand this world he ordered hundreds of Little Blue Books from the Haldemann-Julius people in Kansas, describing the origins of the earth, man and the stars. He read them aloud to his wife. He reflected on their meaning when he worked the plows. When clouds of migrating geese flew over at night he would just fire into the air and pick them up in the morning. His wife boned the flesh, then stored it with the pork in a barrel of fat. When it came time to retire they would go into the mountains where the woods were full of game, and the lakes full of fish, but after six straight years of drought his wife died. He had some pictures taken, postcard size, of himself, which he distributed to friends and interested parties, with words to the effect that he was in the market for a new wife. He sent one to Eddie Cahow, who tucked it into the mirror beside William Jennings Bryan.

THE customer (scented with Cahow's talcum) might admit to a complaint about the weather while he sorted the nails from the coins in his pocket: Cahow might inquire about the health of the missus or the illness of a horse. While he gossiped, chewing on a match, he might adjust his old hat to his new-size head. In the mirror he would take quick stock of his new face. If there were flies trapped in the bulge of the screen he might shoo them out. If he heard the whistle blowing ahead of the train, he might stand as he did in the pew on Sunday, eyes half-lidded, waiting for the sound of the hymn books to close. As the express blasted through, vibrating the windows, rattling the bottles of tonic water, the tremor of the earth would pass like a shiver up and down his legs. He stands and walks like my father, his palms turned backward, invisible weights rounding his shoulders; when he walks, he gives off the sound of a tearing sheet. At high noon he casts a shadow no larger than the brim of his hat. A smokeless flame seems to nibble at its edges and blur the outlines of his horse and buggy, the mare's rump hairless as the breech of a cannon in a city park. Cahow cranks up the chair to watch the dust of the buggy slowly blow out of sight.

At the front of Cahow's shop the half-curtained window frames a portrait of the founding fathers: Hapke, attorney at law, on the east, Nielson, a dealer in cattle and grain, on the west. Sandwiched between, in a room without windows, Doc Toomey lies on a horsehair sofa. He is huge. The door will have to come off when they carry him out. Toomey pulls teeth and sets bones in his office, where the less heard and seen the better. The dim smoking light is green as ditch water from the cracked blind at the door. *Western Adventure* stories are piled high in one corner; a cigar-store wooden Indian stands in another. He smiles with the teeth supplied by Toomey's victims and wears a coonskin cap, a powder horn full of marbles. Boys and girls who lose their teeth—and not their tempers—get a marble from the horn. Women who lose more than they bargained for get from Toomey a glance of melancholy recognition. The giant is soft. He feeds the mice who nest in his unwashed socks. On his desk a jawless pioneer skull holds down a clutter of papers, the crown cleft by the stone ax of an Indian and polished by the palm of Toomey's right hand.

ONCE I found ninety cents in a purse at the Chautauqua and spent all but thirty cents on pop and nut Hersheys. My father felt obliged to thrash me, but he lacked experience and we had no woodshed. He took me into the bedroom, drew the blinds at the windows, the belt from the pants he was wearing, then gripped me by the wrist and around and around we went. He had forgotten, or feared, to drop the seat of my pants, and the leather slapped on the air trapped in my rompers. I could hear him panting. His beltless trousers sagged at his hips. I ran to hide in the piano box behind Eoff's grocery where I made plans to be kidnaped and held for ransom, either by Indians I feared or by gypsies I both feared and admired. Through a knothole in the box I watched my father come out on the screened back porch to cool off, one hand dipped into his pocket to sort out the change that would buy me back. On his next trip to Omaha he would bring me an air gun with a sack of lead BBs that would stick in the barrel or turn up in the crops of Mrs. Riddlemosher's Plymouth Rocks. Run over by a train, BBs come out as thin as tinfoil, but they were not of much use.

PEOPLE will surprise you. Cahow often said so. There was Emil Bickel, a Pennsylvania Dutchman, with everything to live for (a handsome wife and two daughters well married, a son grown old enough to support him) but nothing to die for. He drove a team of roan mares in their Sunday fly nets, hitched to a rubber-tired, red-wheeled buggy, from behind a slow, upgrade freight, moving west, into the path of the ten o'clock Flyer roaring east. Deliberate. He had to stand up in the buggy to keep the team from bolting. Cahow closed his eyes, and when he opened them the Flyer and the buggy were gone. Through the sucked-up cloud of dust, the turbulence of the air, he saw the team dragging their traces in the burned-over ditch grass. On the wires overhead, his arms dangling like a scarecrow, was Emil Bickel in the black suit he reserved for Sundays, the watch in his vest proving the Flyer had hit him right on time. Another man, Karl Anders, walked between the ties with the wind at his back, but Swedes were known to do that. A Bohemian named Hruza was found buried under the fodder in his own silo. A Mrs. Cole—but Cahow needn't dwell on things like that to know people will surprise you. Cahow understood them. There were days he would rather cut a man's hair free than shave his throat.

Cahow had a long view to the west if he inclined his head to where the door screen bulged. Down there the water tank, like a headless bird, the bloody neck still raw and dripping, stood as if the eastbound Flyer had made off with the head like a mail sack. Grass grew where the chute dripped water between the ties. In this short-grass country the only long grass grows where the drip moistens the track cinders. Cahow had once watched a maverick buffalo cropping it up. A big furze-colored bull, high in the shoulders, his short tail wagging like a knotted whip, he had walked along the ties like a country woman with her skirts tucked up. Another time he saw a wolf, crazed by the drought, lick the morning drip from the rails like ice, then chew on the spears of yellow timothy like a dog out of sorts. Another time he saw a coon crawl out on the chute and drink from the spout. On occasion stray geese might circle the tank like a water hole. There was no lack of something to see for a man with the eyes to see it. Gypsies camped down the tracks where the ties were piled and let their horses graze in the ditch grass. The Hagenbeck & Wallace Circus, their painted wagons on the flatcars, parked on the siding near the cattle loader, the summer night filled with the jungle howling of the monkeys, the roar of the cats. An airplane flew out from Omaha and did the loop-the-loop. The greatest orator of his age, William Jennings Bryan, took time out from his campaign for the Presidency of the United States to let Cahow shave him, trim his hair and listen to his advice.

GREAT things were prophesied at the turn of the century. There would be a grove of trees with a Civil War cannon, a bandstand for the grownups, for the kids a drinking fountain that wouldn't hose them when they stooped for a drink. South of the tracks a three-story hotel with the rooms at the front with running water, a lobby with a potted palm at the door and hardwood rockers facing the window. Next door a movie palace with a balcony or a new city hall like the one in Tecumseh, a gents' washroom at the bottom, a flag at the top, a lift to take the ladies to the marriage bureau. The new depot would be brick with an iron-rail fence and teeth along the rail to keep the bums from loitering. Trains would stop daily whether or not there was anybody to get on or off. Warning bells would clang. There would be gates at two crossings you could crank up and down. A church of each denomination, a cemetery, a water trough that would second as a fountain, a café with a violin in a glass case that would play by itself. In each house a woman young enough to bear children and one in the kitchen old enough to raise them. Anything else? If it's Sunday, the grind of an ice-cream freezer and a small boy sick from sucking on the rock salt or chewing roofing tar. Other things would have to wait. The good things should come just one at a time.

I HAD it straight from my father that when he was my age he did the work of two men for half the money. Months before he cut himself with his first straight razor he was a dispatcher for the Union Pacific Railroad, his head ticking with the click of the Morse code. He had learned it on his own, listening and gawking at the ticket window, the ticker chirping like crickets trapped in a jar. He wore black sateen dusters to protect his sleeves; his pencils had red caps, like Pullman porters. The purple lead of these pencils left a stain like a birthmark between his lips. My mother was known to complain about the taste of his kiss. My Grandmother looked straight up, my Grandfather looked west, but my father turned and faced east with the century. A man with no taste for liquor, no time for smoking, no interest in gambling, no need for swearing, he kept his own counsel, left religion to the women and talked mostly to himself.

A STRAW-HAIRED, Scandinavian-type woman, Opal Mason often cried when babies were born, girls especially, or when grown men slept with her. Something about the love-making of men struck her as sad. They came to her at night, walking the railroad ties or in the cinders edging the tracks. Seated on her bed they would take off their shoes and tap out the cinders, leave on their socks. They were mostly good, decent, strong, silent, smelly men, and they all seemed to think they would live forever, make love forever, and then like babies drop off to sleep. She never slept herself, since sleeping she could do at another time. In a railroad town she had the tooting engines, the smoking lanterns, the receding caboose lights, and the sleeping grown-up lovers all at one time. It made her sweetly melancholy. It was a great pleasure for her to lie there and cry.

IF LITTLE happened the way Cahow planned it, over the years, nevertheless, things went on happening. He put in electric clippers, a gum ball machine, a radio. He left in the mirror the postcards of the folks who always meant to come back. A baseball team with seven men, including Cahow, consistently beat a nine-man team from Aurora, the pitcher going all the way and the catcher playing without a mask. The water-pressure system proved to be so expensive the order for the fire-hose cart was canceled. One church, one doctor and one barber proved to be enough. On the Fourth of July that Dempsey whipped Carpentier, Cahow did twenty-three shaves and seventeen haircuts, but it never crossed his mind to get a big head and put in another chair. In the depression he trimmed a lady's hair for a dozen fresh eggs. No one he knew personally accepted free money from the WPA. Every year more of the legs of the trapeze artist peeled from the poster on the water-wagon sprinkler, gobbled up by the man-eating tiger on the one beneath. One thing didn't change. All the screen door did was trap the flies in the shop. If he cranked down the chair and faced the mirror, he noticed the glare less from the street. Some fool kid didn't rap on the window if he happened to doze off. It seemed only yesterday he woke up hearing the church bells signaling the end of the First World War, which Mrs. Cahow thought was announcing the end of the world. "Nellie," he told her, "you live long enough and one day you'll be right."

WHAT made the house a home was the run-around porch, a screen that stuck or slammed, a wire basket of dead ferns, a swing that scuffed the paint off the clapboards, a rail to lean on when you threw up, a stoop to sit on when you watered the grass. Under the stoop you'll find a scooter made of one skate, a wooden-runner sled, a pair of stilts, an iron wheel rim and a stick to push it, parts of an Irish Mail, parts of a tricycle, a cigar box full of tinfoil worth eight cents a pound. Light comes in through the crisscross of slats on the side. A boy seated in the soft, powdery dust can see out better than you can see in. He goes there to pee, fizz up strawberry pop or just think. Time does not fly, or lose itself, or turn to money, or tick like a watch. Time blurs the wheel of a passing buggy or blackens the coal on the locomotive tender where it also spills like water from the lowered chute. There is no end of it. The Jewel's Tea wagon stops where the horse crops the ditch grass, his brown hide twitching under the fly net, the sparrows feeding on the steaming manure in the wagon's shade.

WHERE there was little to see, Cahow saw the most. The mirror framed the scenic props of his mind. Right at the moment the plain grew dark, the sky filled with light. It was there after the sun had set in the evening, and it would be there when he arose in the morning, as if this light were a property of the sky itself, the moon, as much as the sun, the source of it. In the dusk the bats winged in and out of the stable as if it were dark, their radar clicking, and at this time in the evening lost coins came out to be found. The tracks to the east gleamed like ice in the cinders, and the locomotive headlight smoked like a comet. If a grass fire had been smoldering during the day, he would watch the flames flicker at night, and smoke from these fires never left the bedroom of his house. His wife shook the dust out of the curtains, but the smell of the grass fire lingered. Cahow grew to like it. It seemed to be trapped in the wings of his nose. He had read or heard somewhere that a great sheet of ice had scoured the plain like a snowplow. The sea had lapped it. The dinosaur had wallowed in it like a hog. Little wonder that his eyes seemed so wet although his tongue was dry as a cob, or that he heard water lapping like the reins on the rump of a horse.

Some things were slow to change. Dirty-minded little boys played with themselves under porches or ran hooting like Indians with their pants unbuttoned or stood around under the fire escape on the school building or hid in old piano boxes to smoke punk and corn silk. Evil-mouthed older boys drew dirty pictures in the privies or wrote foul-mouthed sayings on the sides of freight cars with Kewpie chalk. The girls were better, with chores to keep them busy, but they let themselves get cornered in rented buggies, or where the weeds were high behind the Chautauqua, or in the back of a movie, or in the loft of a barn, or in the sag of a hammock, or in the willows near the river, there being no place on earth some evil-minded galoot couldn't trap a dumb girl. Which naturally led to more kids, some of them boys, with nothing on their evil little minds but girls, and girls who seemed to know nothing but what a boy had on his mind. How they ever grew up God only knew, but once they did they proved to be like the others, decent, law-abiding people with another crop of evil-minded kids.

I WAS not one of those kids, but I showed promise. One of them said to me, "I saw U.P. on a freight car." On the small hole in the three-seater privy I brooded on their verse and studied their drawings. I knew why the spring seats were often missing from the buggies, and where to look for hairpins where the grass was trampled. I gave it some thought. I used to swing with my romper seat flapping, pee'd pop into bottles, pee'd life into house plants, rain barrels and the ferns dying on porches, wrestled with Evelyn Clarke and fought with Vance Fry because of what he called my mother. I did not play with my pecker out of fear that Dr. Toomey would cut it off. I found a tin of balloons in my father's pocket and filled them with water, but I was not precocious: I had seen it done. To impress Dean Cole I dipped my head into a tar barrel, but entirely on my own I learned to eat raw cookies, nibble on cow pies, suck up rain water through a toy train wheel, ride a bike side-saddle, dye rotten eggs for Easter, and smoke Fourth of July punk dipped in coal oil. My eye to the knothole in the Riddlemosher privy, Dean Cole scored a bull's-eye in the freckles just beneath it, but I saved the BB and shot it back into the seat of his pants.

ONE expected something better of a child of my mother, but on my father's side I come from people. Lots of them. Eleven sons and three daughters were born and raised in Ohio, but not all of the boys were home for the picture. The girls had married: they are the ones without the mustaches. My Uncle Harry slid his glasses down his nose and said, "Lord, it's fadin'."

"Most of them dead and gone," Clara said. "Think it would be fadin'."

"Come to think," he said, "they never had much as faces." He wheeled around in the chair. "That's Mitchell." He put a finger on him. "Just died over east of Sioux City." He wheeled back and wagged a finger through the doorway. "May's in Falls City. Indian country. Man she married rode around all night in a mail car. When they stopped in Lincoln, found him dead in it."

"All that jigglin'," Clara said, "didn't help him any."

He wheeled to face the piano. "Emerson's out in Cozad. All girls in his family."

"Had pictures on the wall he hand-painted," said Clara.

"One of a dog you'd swear he'd come right down and bite you."

"Last time we saw him he was spry as a kid."

"And now he's gone."

"Way we'll all soon be gone," Clara said.

WHILE still a boy, my Uncle Verne was mistaken for a man by the Canadian Army, which he joined in order to shoot a gun. He was gassed at Verdun and came back on a stretcher. His own sister hardly recognized him. He was bald, had the twitches and a government pension. He wore a black fedora hat with a wide limp brim, a blue serge suit and hook-and-eye shoes. There were grass stains on his knees and the crease of bench slats across his back. He carried his own tin cup, a straight-blade razor, and a Nabisco cookie tin he kept his cigars in. My father tried to interest him in a sound business venture, but Uncle Verne wasn't cut out for business. He liked jelly beans and banana candy. He liked me and kids. He had been through the war, but it was my father who scared him to death. He liked to ride in the front seat of the Studebaker over the new gravel road between Omaha and Fremont, the side curtains flapping, my father asleep in the wide back seat. At turns in the road he liked to look back and see the blue exhaust. It's not accurate to say he was never again heard from since he sent me a postcard from Melbourne. I lost it before I knew how far away it was. One of my aunts sends him cards at Christmas in care of his Social Security number, and he must be around somewhere because she sends them first class and they never come back.

ONE of the girls married an Elliot and went east to Virginia. Harry thinks it was Olive. Clara knows it was Mabel. The man she married died since she later remarried. You can't keep track of people if you don't so much as know their proper names.

ONE of the boys ended up in Colorado. He did water drilling and worked for the railroad. He never married. He sometimes wrote to May, the sister he felt close to. If he knew little else, he knew his own mind. That was what people said.

FRANCENA ended up before you could say she had begun. Over near Loup City in the rolling country the government put aside for the Indians. The Sioux Nation. Nice and social as you please. Boys with those high cheekbones, girls with the long black hair. A cousin of Mitchell's wife married one of them. Francena taught in a school where they were all asked to come with handkerchiefs over their faces to keep out the flu germs. A lot of good it did them. Some said they caught it from the army mules. She wouldn't have died if she had listened to Clara and come to live on the farm till the flu was over. They burned only clean white cobs in the range. They kept out the night air. In Uncle Harry's opinion, Francena's trouble stemmed from the way she slept with the windows open, the damp night air like so much water on her lungs.

AGAINST the night air of the early morning Clara wore a man's sweater she never buttoned, the sleeves rolled on her forearms, a stocking cap pulled over her ears. Glass eggs to give the slow hens a timely suggestion weighted the pockets of the sweater; from one arm dangled the Karo syrup pail she used to collect the eggs. She was at home in the cold but ill at ease with the comfortable. A tall lath-flat woman, she crossed the chicken-pitted yard like an ostrich accustomed to the soft spots. Once a week she baked bread and once a month she baked pies that turned moss-green stored in the storm cave, then turned back to pies when she wiped them with a cloth dipped in vinegar. In the winter she painted back on the linoleum the pattern she had worn off over the summer. She moved her rocker from the front room to keep it from wearing a hole in the rug. Under the lines where the wash dripped were two bent-over wickets and a croquet ball split like an apple. She used the croquet mallet to set out stakes for her tomatoes and club a bull snake to death that was pestering her chickens, but in general she frowned on violence and games. She used Harry's checkers to keep the cream separator level, and Mae's caroms to keep the table on casters from tipping. Clara would rather just sit, fanning herself with her apron, or sorting the hen-spotted eggs from the clean ones, than be caught dead or alive playing dominoes. If they turned up in her clothespins, it was none of her business and she couldn't care less.

THERE's little to see, but things leave an impression. It's a matter of time and repetition. As something old wears thin or out, something new wears in. The handle on the pump, the crank on the churn, the dipper floating in the bucket, the latch on the screen, the door on the privy, the fender on the stove, the knees of the pants and the seat of the chair, the handle of the brush and the lid to the pot exist in time but outside taste; they wear in more than they wear out. It can't be helped. It's neither good nor bad. It's the nature of life.

PROPPED on her arms at the sink, propped on her legs at the stove, propped on both legs and arms, one hand clutching a mop rag, or spread flat on her back clutching the bed frame, Clara knew the sin of idleness and the holiness of work. Seated with the levers of her limbs folded, she continued to rock, a machine idling, an engine with a head of steam faintly hissing, a pendulum of forces, a marvel of devices, finely ground as a lens and honed to a knife's edge, fit to the daily tasks like a work glove. Harry's wife and my Aunt Clara was the triumph of the form following function, the function followed to its end.

LOVE, too, was work, childbirth its reward, a task to be performed like seedtime and harvest, the labor pains what it cost you for the pleasure that couldn't be helped. One paid for the miracle of life with the labor of death. Not everyone had a talent for it, or understood it should not come easy. A man should be long suffering, his death long remembered, the funeral a consecrated working party with the shovel handles sticking out of the raw mounds of earth. Over the wide valley a dim thin rain, the bluffs along the river grained like clapboards, the prevailing wind blowing a cloudlike mist along the tracks. The sleeting rain should glisten on the bared heads of the men and drip from the chins of those still beardless, their prayers rising skyward but their eyes on the hole in the earth. They stand tilted on the boards edging the grave and as the first spade of earth falls hollow on the coffin let it be the one moment in their lives they will never forget.

O<small>N HIS</small> sand farm near Norfolk my Uncle Harry went in for what he called dry farming. He planted corn, wheat, alfalfa and cottonwood trees. The trees did pretty well. They shaded the path all the way to the pasture, along which, on the canter, I brought in the cows. Most of the year Uncle Harry milked the herd, but during my visits it wasn't worth the trouble. After the run I gave them they all ran a little dry. I brought them in on the gallop, mooing like crazy, their tails up like tassels, their udders heavy with buttermilk on the hoof. In the dark stable the squirt drummed in the pail. The sound of it brought the cats on the double to sit in the doorway, or press against the walls, where Uncle Harry would try to squirt them between the eyes. The smart cats would let it spatter on their fronts, then lick it off. *Warm milk from the titty made a cat purty*. That was what he said. He let the kittens lick the froth from the fingers he dipped in the pail. In the twilight the bats flickered over the yard and the salt lick in the corral gleamed like a snow cake. Across the darkening yard, submerged in the shadows, the croquet post tilted like a grave marker, and I knew where the wickets were trampled in the grass like booby traps. I couldn't see the water pumped into the pail, but I knew when it was full by the sound of it. Because the wire pail handle cut into my palm I would stop and switch hands at the cobhouse, the water I spilled wetting the weeds between the cracks of the stoop. So Harry wouldn't spill her milk Clara would stand waiting for him at the open screen.

HE SAID "sye" for "says I," "see" for "says he," smoked Old Whale on weekdays, Union Leader on Sundays, chewed Mail Pouch, snuffed Copenhagen, suffered from a weight at the pit of his stomach, liked berry pie, oatmeal cooked till you could stretch it, vulcanized eggs, coffee with canned cream, fresh store bread, Senator Capper, barrel candy with the soft centers, Teddy Roosevelt, Billy Sunday, and this big local fellow Dempsey over that little French fellow Carpenteer. He cleaned eggs with his thumbnail, sat on the nails in his pockets, left his spoon in the sugar, left the flies in the dipper, left the mice in the cobs, the apples on the tree, the grapes on the vine, his hat on his head, the harrow in the yard, and the door to the privy standing open, his breath smoking in the winter air, the sun warm on his knees. He paid me ten cents a bushel for shelling his popcorn and once traveled, with other dry farmers, free in both directions, in a private car supplied by the implement dealers, from Omaha to Des Moines, where he gave his opinion that no fool gas tractor would replace the horse. In the summer he liked a straw with a shadow he could stand in, in the winter underwear he could sleep in, but he never gave an inkling if he liked or didn't like the woman he married.

He was like weeds in the spring, corn over the summer, hay in the fall, manure over the winter and a sack of grain after Sunday dinner. He was strong as a horse, stubborn as a mule, slow as molasses, smart as a whip, but what there was that was human in his nature was slow to emerge. His roots were long, but not much showed above the ground. His home-grown virtues were anesthetic: they killed pain by drugging his feelings. His eyes were wide open, but his nerves were numb. He had a good word for horses and other people's children, a knowledge of livestock, a reckoning for dead stock, an elephant's memory, an old hen's bottom and a pullet's scratch. Half an hour before sunrise he heard on the wireless that this fellow Truman had beaten Governor Dewey. At breakfast he said aloud, "He's not my man, but he's my President." After breakfast he did the chores, patched a hole in the screen, patched a hole in a tube, wired the seat of the harrow, straightened a prong of the fork, sharpened the hoe, used the dipper to skim the flies off the pail, filled his pipe with Old Whale and scratched a kitchen match on a lid of her stove.

HARRY's boy, Will, went to the state's Aggie College, where he unlearned what little the old man had taught him. He was like Clara, raw-boned, knobby and stubborn, his Adam's apple so big his neck looked bent. Using a little fertilizer and hybrid corn, Will averaged about forty bushels of corn to the acre. Using the experience of forty-five years and the rheumatism that tipped him off about the weather, Harry averaged up to fifteen bushels to the acre, if the weather was good. Will also managed to build himself a house that Harry said looked like a caboose on a siding. It set up high like that to make room for the furnace he could sit with his feet on most of the winter. In the summer he put a trailer on the rear of his pickup and just let his farm sit while he drove around the country. The kids, of course, liked it. His wife mailed Clara a postcard from Yellowstone Park. Will's wife got along just fine with Harry, but Will never again set foot in the old man's house, ate a bite of his food or borrowed his harrow or corn planter. He said it was easier to buy himself a new one than dig the old one out of the weeds. Through the screen of box elders, on a summer night, you could see Harry reading his *Capper's Weekly*, or turn and see his son Will listening to the Lone Ranger cry "Heigh-ho, Silver!" That's what comes from sending a boy away to Aggie College or anywhere else.

WILL married Nora Hadley, a girl he met at the Polzen reunion, where she won the cake-bake and he won the sack race. Harry said he would have as soon gone to her funeral. They were married in Indian summer weather in a church too small for both families. Through the wide-open doors she could see the teams drawn up under the elms. One of her people stood combing the seeds and burrs from a white mare's tail. It was quiet in the hollow, but on the rise a westerly breeze turned the wheel of a windmill. Through its spinning blades, like a swirl of water, she could see the granite stones in the cemetery, the names blurred by the wagging shadows of the long-stemmed grass. A man walked between the stones, swinging a scythe. The cutting sound was like a seam pulled from a dress or the rip of a flour sack torn up for dish towels. She watched him work his way like Father Time to where he paused in the shade to hone the blade with a stone from his pocket, a rasping sound like a cow scratching on a taut wire. Near the windmill a farmer was sinking a post with the noise of jug corks popping, the stubbled field blackened with a throng of cawing crows. In the pause that his hammer hung in the air her new life had begun.

CLARA's daughter, Janet, married Ivy Cable, a Battle Creek boy. She gave more time to her Leghorns than to her husband and children and let her food sit cold while she listened to Lowell Thomas. Ivy learned to like it cold. In the winter she ordered and read all the free government pamphlets and sat up half the night around the incubator. When the chicks hatched out, she let them mess and chirp all over the place. She put in electric power, an inside toilet, bought a washer, a drier and a freezer on credit, then taught school for eight years just to get, as she said, out of the house. She used her bony finger to poke you in the breastbone when she talked. Both she and her husband liked the barrel cookies without the icing, and Christmas hard candy with the soft centers, but Janet didn't think the candy was the same as when she was a girl. She actually thought it was better. She drove Clara crazy with that kind of talk.

ALTHOUGH a city-bred man, Ivy liked nothing better than to hand-shell his own popcorn, hand-crank his own ice cream, and use the outdoor facilities the house came with rather than the new one they put in the basement. Ivy had started from scratch with a popcorn wagon featuring a toy clown that poured butter on the popcorn, a piston hissing as a real toy steam engine did the work. When he graduated to an ice-cream parlor with wire-backed chairs, he didn't let success spoil him. He liked to eat well, but he never lost his taste for day-old cornbread with Carnation milk on it. He didn't like it thinned with water, like Janet. First he crumbled up the cornbread in a tall glass, then he poured on the milk, right from the can, using the handle of a soda spoon to slush it up and down. Every year he took the family to Omaha and put up in a hotel during Ak-Sar-Ben Week (Nebraska spelled backward), but nothing pleased him more than to pee from the porch into a fresh fall of snow.

IF THE days happened to fall when she had the time to spare, Clara observed both the holidays and the Sabbath. She preferred the Sabbath. The drive to Battle Creek was longer and gave her more time to think. She had been baptized a Lutheran back in Salem, but she felt that she was lacking in religious faith. Religious feeling she had; the singing of the choir brought a lump to her throat. She would stand holding the hymnal, not singing herself, her eyes on the head of Mrs. Eiseley's fur piece, the tail wagging while she pedaled the organ with her rubbers on. What she lacked in religious faith she tried to make up in observance. If Harry could hitch up the buggy, they were always there in the pew. If there was one thing she would change if she could do it all over, she would put the front door of the house at the back and not have let her daughter Mae have the piano. She missed not seeing it there in the parlor, the music open on the rack.

WHEN the land across the road was put up for sale, one of Harry's cousins bought it. He liked to fish. He didn't really need a woman around the house. He'd rather ride his Ranger bike into town than hitch up the horse. When he came home after dark he'd rather undress in the dark than fool around with the lamp. There were things on his mind. He seemed to think about them better if the room was dark. He kept the green blinds drawn against the winter light but he could still make out the tilted mirror on the bureau, the iron frame of the bed and the picture of wild horses on the lid covering the stove-pipe hole. The veneer on the bureau was of bird's-eye maple, but in the dark this was lost on him. In the top drawer of the bureau, rolled up inside out, he kept his socks. The bottle of cherry cough syrup beside the clock was less for his cough than his upset stomach. He swigged it from the bottle; he said it sealed his lips shut till he woke up. The only sound in his house was when he dropped his shoes on the floor. Kids were crazy about Ed, the girls especially, and he liked to taunt them with a poem he recited:

> I'd be a single man,
> Jolly and free,
> I'd be a bachelor,
> With a latchkey.

It did no good to remind him that he had no reason to lock an empty house.

ONCE a day, from where he leaned in the window, Ed could watch the Burlington come down from the north, the pistons hissing and the black smoke pouring from the funnel stack. As she came around the curve, the bell rocking, the fireman would leave the engine cab for the tender, and scramble over the coal to the lid on the water bin. The Burlington took on water at the station, and the fireman had to be there to lower the stack. If the wind was right Ed could hear the water spilling into the chute. While the engine sat there the bell would clang and the pistons would steam up the bricks along the platform. Ed couldn't see it, but he knew it from experience. As a kid he had liked the feel of the moist warm bricks on his bare feet. When the train pulled out he could see the crossing gates bob on the sky. The man who cranked them up, Mr. Riddlemosher, would wave Ed through if all he had with him was his bike. Once he saw this butterfly on the cowcatcher. He was still there when the train pulled out and might have had himself a free ride all the way to Aurora. It was not unusual for birds to fly in and out of the caboose. Until it was winter Ed didn't happen to notice the dark rings worn into the bark on his two white birch trees: in the spring he saw they were made by hammock ropes. Ed had the type of mind that wouldn't rest till he had puzzled such things out.

THE MAN who lives his own life, and wears it out, can dispense with the need of taking it with him. He dies his own death or he goes on living, and where the life has worn in the death will come out. Skin and bones, jacket and shoes, tools, sheds and machines wear out; even the land wears out and the seat wears off the cane-bottom chair. The palms wear off the gloves, the cuffs off the sleeves, the nickel off the doorknobs, the plate off the silver, the flowers off the plates, the shine off the stovepipe, the label off the flour sacks, the enamel off the dipper, the varnish off the checkers, and the gold off the Christmas jewelry, but every day the nap wears off the carpet the figure wears in. A pattern for living, the blueprint of it, can be seen in the white stitches of the denim, the timepiece stamped like a medallion in the bib of the overalls. Between wearing something in and wearing it out the line is as vague as the receding horizon, and as hard to account for as the missing hairs of a brush. The figure that began on the front of the carpet has moved around to the back.

In the middle of life my father gave up his chance to be a chief dispatcher for the Union Pacific Railroad, in order to start a chicken farm with three thousand Leghorns laying fresh eggs daily. The chickens would lay the eggs at night so the Pullman diners could have them in the morning. My father's day-old eggs would be on the diner tables in Chicago and Salt Lake. Nobody told my father what he was in for once he started fooling around with chickens. His brother Harry could have told him, but my father didn't ask. One day you find one droopy. In the next day or two you find half of them dead. Especially Leghorns. Once the cholera got into them they were as good as gone.

From the second-floor window where my father had locked me with a dog named Shep and a woman named Gertrude, we watched the fenced-in farm turn white with sick chickens. People drove out from town to sit in their buggies and watch them die. Sick chickens like to find a place where they can huddle, and they lined the fence like drifted snow. The live ones huddled on the dead ones, and those that weren't dead smothered. A pit was dug in the field where my father had planted beans as his contribution to the war effort, and they filled it with dead chickens, shoveled on the quicklime and covered them up. But in any batch of chickens there's always a few that refuse to die. About fifty did, three of them roosters that crowed every morning as if they were healthy. My father put them in coops and sent them to his brother Harry, who refused to pick them up on the railroad platform. My father had to pay the freight and have them shipped back before they starved to death.

THE DOG named Shep had come with the chicken farm, but my father had brought me a spring-wind train, a Ouija board and a new mother from Omaha. "Son," he had said to me, "come and kiss your new mother." While my father sat up nights with the incubators, my new mother and I worked the Ouija board or played records on her new Victrola. Her name was Gertrude. She liked "When you wore a tulip, a bright yellow tulip." I liked "Stop Your Ticklin', Jock." She was eight years older than I was, and fatter, but we were almost equal wrestling. I beat her at caroms. She beat me at parcheesi. She had been a cigar-counter girl at the Winslow Hotel where she played dice with the men for cigars. Because my father didn't smoke she played for me and won. That was what she said. We got along fine. It was my father who didn't get along so well with us. While he looked for a new home for us to move into, we went to matinees at the Empress, drank cherry phosphates and rode the moving stairs at Burgess & Nash. People thought we were both my father's children and advised him to send us to a good school somewhere, one that would keep us both, especially her, off the streets.

IT WAS not right for Gertrude, but I was enrolled in Mrs. Partridge's class at Farnam School. In the morning we pledged allegiance to the American flag and exercised to the music of "The Clock Store." The exercises began fast, then got slower and slower as the Victrola ran down. If we all wrote on the blackboard at the same time, the chalk dust in the air gave Mrs. Partridge splitting headaches. The squeak of the chalk put her nerves on edge and she would have to lie down in the nurse's annex, a towel over her eyes. On the stairs we had to be careful not to step on the tassels of her shawl. After school Betty Zabriskie, Byron Minter and me would clean the basket of erasers at the fire-escape window, slapping them on the bricks. The chalk dust made your fingers squeaky and whitened the bricks around the fire-escape window. In the classroom picture taken the day it rained the colored boys didn't show unless they wore white shirts. Mrs. Partridge, Vance Fry and Joey Mulligan moved and came out blurred. In a letter to my father Mrs. Mulligan said that what an orphan child needed was a home and a mother. My father agreed. Gertrude had left him to become a hula dancer with three Hawaiians. Along with me to the Mulligans came the living room suite, from storage, Gertrude's walnut Victrola, five Harry Lauder records, and a packet of used needles someone had mixed with the good ones just out of spite.

A BLACK man swept the station where my father worked and stoked the furnace where I went to school. He rang the bell at recess and shoveled snow off the front and rear steps. A black man owned a mule that wore a hat in the summer and was as smart, it was said, as he was. A black boy delivered laundry, washed and ironed by his mother, summer and winter on a wooden-runner sled. I never saw her. They lived behind the cattle loader down the Burlington tracks. Black faces could be seen through the wide diner windows when the Overland Express stopped for water, and white jackets and white smiles flashed between the passing coaches. They were all God's chillun, but it was my country, not theirs. In Mrs. Partridge's class a boy sat beside me black as the bottom side of a stove lid. I did most of his fractions. He won all of my marbles. More white than black, taller than my father, Edward Dorsey had to sit without a bench to write on, his knees in the aisles, his baseball glove looped to his belt. He could throw a ball so fast the batters couldn't see it and nobody could catch it. He had been in the seventh grade two years and liked it best. There were also Lily, Mike, Eleanor and Larue, but only Edward Dorsey showed up clear in the picture, his head like a paper cutout among the pumpkins in the kindergarten window. They were all the chillun of some other country the Lord would provide.

AFTER working all night getting out the morning paper Mr. Mulligan tried to sleep in the bedroom off the kitchen. Joey and me slept in the parlor on the sofa that opened out at night. To help the goldfish sleep, the bowl was covered with a sugar sack. The folding doors between the rooms were opened wide on Sunday when Mr. Mulligan smoked his White Owl in the parlor, read his *Popular Mechanics* and measured a hair from somebody's head with his micrometer. Otherwise the doors were closed and we carried our shoes down the hallway to the kitchen before we put them on. Mrs. Mulligan only put on her shoes when she sat on the porch. She wore stockings to keep the linoleum pattern off the bottom of her feet. Sometimes Mr. Mulligan arrived home with the milkman and they came down the hill together, the horse clopping, the bottles clinking when the milkman whistled or the horse came to a halt. Mrs. Mulligan liked to iron in the cool of the morning, in just her slip. She would put up the board in the door of the pantry, where the scorched smell of the pad would blow on the draft. In the afternoon Mr. Mulligan would shave at the window he'd let down from the top. If we were coming down the alley, we could see his lathered face. He had played pro ball with the Mineola Redbirds, and you could see the Redbird stamped on the sweatshirt he wore on those days he liked to play a little catch.

ONE SUNDAY in Duluth Mrs. Mulligan's three brothers took her and her friend Dora Eigner out rowing. Andrew and Lyle rowed. From out on the water Mrs. Mulligan could see this boy with the light tan shoes on the pier. That was Mr. Mulligan. When their time was up and they came in with the boat, he cried, "The one with the green parasol for me!" That was her. Her name was Flora Lindgren then, but not for long. They were married in Minneapolis, then went to Salt Lake, where they opened an ice-cream parlor. Mr. Mulligan made the ice cream so rich it waxed the roof of everybody's mouth. In Omaha she never wanted to see ice cream again. Mr. Mulligan made home brew in the crock in the pantry, and in a fit of rage, brought on when the crock broke, he threw Joey through the pantry window into the yard, where the sand put there for paving the alley saved his life. Now he was bigger than his mother. If big feet meant anything, he would be a big man.

M<small>Y FEET</small> were not big. My knee pants were always below my knees. I preferred to ride a man's bike side-saddle, the sprocket wearing a grease spot on one shin, and my father often wondered what was on my mind. He spoke to Mrs. Healy, in the eighth grade, about it, and she referred him to *Tom Sawyer*. In case I might be too smart for Tom Sawyer, she gave him three books by Ralph Henry Barbour. My father read them late at night, in the bathroom, or in the egg-candling room of his produce business, using the light that came through the holes of the candler. If he could believe what he read, all I had on my mind was good clean fun. All I wanted to do was pitch the winning game and win the cross-country run. That seemed a long way to run, but my father believed that I could. Later he hoped to send me to an Eastern school where I would live in a room hung with college pennants, and spend Christmas with my roommate whose younger sister was home from her boarding school. Playing run-sheep-run at night with Lillian Eichler, we stood holding hands in Mrs. Seidel's coal bin, where my breathing was noisy but I had no idea what was on my mind.

Mr. Lockwood, of Spalding Bros., knew what was on my mind even better than I did. He sold my father a Louisville slugger bat with a roll of tape to put on the handle, plus an official ball and a catcher's mask, so I could take part in the national pastime. My father had no objection if I would wear the mask and play out in left field where I wouldn't get hurt. Mr. Lockwood had once been a great athlete himself and run the quarter-mile as fast as any man alive. You wouldn't think it to look at him, but he had been a track star at an eastern college. In a compartment of his wallet he had a packet of clippings showing how he had looked and how fast he had run. It seemed hard to believe that Mr. Lockwood was the same man. He had run the quarter-mile in forty-nine seconds flat, which was as far, or farther, than four city blocks. He had come back later and helped four of his teammates run a whole mile. Everything Mr. Lockwood said about boys confirmed what my father had read in the books. If he had been a writer, Mr. Lockwood might have written them all himself. Listening to him, my father could see very clearly the wonderful world that lay behind Mr. Lockwood, but it was difficult to see what it was that lay ahead. His son had run off and got married, giving his father no inkling of what was on his mind.

A SUMMER twilight Mr. Mulligan told us about life. We had been playing catch and sat along the curb watching the bats dip in and out of the shadows; we were waiting for the lamplighter to come along and light up the street. A conspiracy of loose women (Mr. Mulligan told us), in particular waitresses and movie ushers, accosted small boys of our clean-cut type in the balcony seats of cheap movie houses, bicycle shops and behind old billboards. We should take special caution whenever we went to pee. (This spoke to me, as I had a thing going with several old billboards.) Another danger was the lecherous old men who asked boys if they'd like to see a movie, or gave you a quarter for doing no more than delivering a note. (I had done that. I took the money, that is, but chickened out when I saw the stairs were dark.) Just in passing, Mr. Mulligan warned us that to sit too long on a concrete curb might give you the piles. Waitresses and old men with a letch for small boys I soon learned to take in my lengthening stride, but I have never been able, without dark foreboding, to sit long on a curb.

On Halloween Mr. Pilsenki chased us up and down the alleys, across the weeded empty lots, between the dark tilting houses, to where, because he was a giant, he swung by his neck on Mrs. Goodman's clothesline. On the Fourth of July Mr. Ahearn set fire to Mrs. Seidel's curtains with a Roman candle, and Mr. Mulligan, using sparklers, lost his eyebrows lighting dead firecrackers. Jews were dirty, Polacks were dumb, but they were next-door neighbors and fun to play with. When Charlie Schulz died, only Joey Mulligan had a blue serge suit and could be a pallbearer. In the clothes closet off the nurse's annex I sat in the dark on Mrs. Healy's galoshes, breathing in the smell of the raincoat she had left on the hook. In the dark of this closet I acquired a new mother, a pair of chain-tread bike tires, relations I would have to take a train ride to visit, and a nonmagnetic gold-filled watch from Santa Claus, signed "Love from your Dad." On Twenty-fourth and Farnam, where I sold papers, he whistled to me from a Studebaker Six with side curtains. It was like being kidnaped. It began a new life for both of us. He left behind him more than five coops of live chickens, and I left behind me a Flexible Flyer, a cigar box full of marbles, and the pocket torn from Babe Ruth's barnstorming pants, all under the dangerous steps at the front of the Mulligan house.

For my father, *up ahead* was Chicago. He never mentioned New York. The map on the wall of the small-town depot, and the map on the wall of the big-city lobby, showed the chicken-track lines, tangled like mop strings, that led to and away from Chicago. That's where everything seemed to come from, and most things ended up. To get the feel of the city, as well as see where you are going, it's best to stand with the motorman at the front of the streetcar and ride north, twenty minutes or so, toward Lincoln Park. There's a bar rail at his back you can get a good grip on. There's a breath of hot or cool air when he opens the doors. The street smells by itself in the summer, but in the winter, when the tracks are icy, the flinty smell of crushed sand comes up through the floor when the car starts and stops. At the street intersections you can look to the west, and the miles and miles of slums, or you can look to the east, where the world seems to end. The great lake is down there, along with the homes of the rich. There's a bridle path that runs along under the trees, and between the legs of the horses with their braided tails you can see the lake. After working all night, sorting waybills, my father liked to walk along the bridle-path cinders. In the cool dawn light he might be mistaken for one of the rich. He greeted those on horseback who had nothing to do in this world but ride. Men who lived in Waukegan, driven to work by chauffeurs, saw my father as one of the money barons out for a relaxing walk before assuming the burdens of wealth.

BABBITT

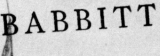

CHAPTER I

I

THE towers of Zenith aspired above the morning mist; austere towers of steel and cement and limestone, sturdy as cliffs and delicate as silver rods. They were neither citadels nor churches, but frankly and beautifully office-buildings.

The mist took pity on the fretted structures of earlier generations: the Post Office with its shingle-tortured mansard, the red brick minarets of hulking old houses, factories with stingy and sooted windows, wooden tenements colored like mud. The city was full of such grotesqueries, but the clean towers were thrusting them from the business center, and on the farther hills were shining new houses, homes—they seemed —for laughter and tranquillity.

Over a concrete bridge fled a limousine of long sleek hood and noiseless engine. These people in evening clothes were returning from an all-night rehearsal of a Little Theater play, an artistic adventure considerably illuminated by champagne. Below the bridge curved a railroad, a maze of green and crimson lights. The New York Flyer boomed past, and twenty lines of polished steel leaped into the glare.

In one of the skyscrapers the wires of the Associated Press were closing down. The telegraph operators wearily raised their celluloid eye-shades after a night of talking with Paris and Peking. Through the building crawled the scrubwomen, yawning, their old shoes slapping. The dawn mist spun away.

MY FATHER worked nights in order to have the day to himself. In the afternoon he read the want ads, and considered Business Opportunities Offered. He spent the night sorting waybills in the freight yards between the drainage canal and Halsted Street. When a boat honked on the canal the drawbridge would go up, the lanterns topping the span rising like planets. The smoking lights of the traffic piled up behind it, glowing red as the door to a furnace. The clamor and tooting were like that of an army at the castle gates. With the bridge up the tower room was my father's castle, the canal was his moat. He experienced peculiar feelings. He sometimes thought himself the last man in the world. Alone in the tower room he was free to think his own thoughts. Over the roofs of the city, beyond the stench of the canal, the floodlights glowed on the Wrigley Tower, and the Palmolive beacon flecked the sky like northern lights. The names on the freight cars, like those on the waybills, moved across his dreaming mind like music, or the glowworm that danced from word to word in the popular song.

THE EL DORADO & WESTERN, the Bauxite & Northern, or the Tucson, Cornelia & Gila Bend, the Genesee & Wyoming, the Lackawanna & Western, the Atchison, Topeka & Santa Fe. The long night's work emptied him of the present but filled him with the past. He could gaze down the long, dark lanes of the freight cars to where a flare hissed and smoked, or a semaphore beckoned, or a brakeman rocked his lantern like a muted or distant crossing bell. At the end of the line my father found all the lines loose in his lap. He could ravel or unravel the threads of his life. He worked nights in order to have daytime on his hands. In the hotel lobby, or on the grass of the park, he could spell out his plans for the future, based, as they were, on his indestructible past. Most men seemed to share it. Little if anything needed to be explained. Small towns proved to be where everybody was from. The bigger the man, as a rule, the smaller the town. With that understood, the smallest town of all was the town of the man to whom you were speaking. It might be Sharon Springs in western Kansas...

Or it might be French Lick in southern Indiana, or no town at all, just the biggest little place on God's green earth. It was amazing how many people proved to be from somewhere else. "I see here," one says, "it's ninety-eight in Kansas," and taps with his finger on the item in the *Tribune*. To top that you point out what it is in South Dakota, or, better yet, what it was last week in Oklahoma. At the counter in the restaurant, at your side on the streetcar, at your elbow on the corner, at your ear on the bench, there was a man or a woman whose brother or sister either knew or married one of your cousins. As a boy you saw the name on a lumber-yard fence, or like a signal at the top of a grain elevator: T. B. HORDE. Until they painted it over you knew that was where he was. It seemed impossible to believe that a town so big could be put together out of places so small. One thing leads to another, but once you're in Chicago everything leads back to where you came from, wherever that was.

Wᴵᵀᴴ ᴹᴱ in mind, my father picked a room with a view of the park. From the window, if the trees were bare, we could lean out and see the statue of Lincoln, green as the bent prong of the fork used to open the hole in a can of milk. In the room only one person could dress at a time, but that was no problem since the father worked nights. He was in bed in the morning when the boy got up. It was the sheets that took a beating since there was always someone between them. One day the boy came running up the stairs to find his father seated in the bed spout, where the springs sagged, with a girl in his lap. Her face was like a clown's mask bobbing on his shoulder; her thighs hugged his waist. And the boy had arrived on the scene too late; the machine would not stop. Coins dropped from the man's pockets to roll about on the floor. No, it was not a good scene. It considerably widened the widening gap. The boy was a great one for Sir Gawain, the Green Knight, and feared disease from stool seats and unclean thoughts. He believed in success. Like his father he preferred to undress in the dark. There was not too much of it, thanks to the toothbrush sign that blinked like a beacon on the corner of Sedgwick, or the light in the bathroom across the street. The lower half of the window was painted green, but you could see the head of the person who sat there, or the shape of the woman who put up her arm to grope for the cord.

In the glow of this light the iron frame of the bed was like the scrollwork of a balcony, and my father, his shirt unbuttoned, was a ghost hastily summoned to a séance. He sagged to the bed spout to take off his shoes, then rose, knees flexed, to slip off his pants. In dark or light, winter or summer, my father never departed from the assembly pattern: he hoisted the pants, then let them drop in a puddle to slip on his shirt. The Hitchcock buckle and chain set I had given him for Christmas would keep his Ingersoll watch from falling from his pocket, but the initial belt buckle would thump and drag on the floor. The silver plate would wear off the initial that worked as well for me as it did for him. Pretending sleep, I would calculate whether to wake up and question him about it, or go on sleeping and take it from him by stealth. By stealth was simpler (I replaced it with my old one), and he never missed it. I liked to point out to him, man to man, how a silver initial buckle was lost on a belt covered up with a vest.

In the street below the window the Italian boys who ate the boiled snails bought them in candy-striped bags, like popcorn, fished them out with bent pins, then crunched the empty shells on the walk. At night the shell powder glowed in the street light like the runner of roach poison on the stairs. When the trolley wire flashed, the room across the street was reflected in the tilted bureau mirror, the gas plate, the crumpled bed, the frosted bulb on the cord lumpy with flies. The loud boom at the window, if it was winter, would be a sign of spring and the lake ice cracking; if it was summer, it would mean someone at Wrigley Field had hit a home run. Winter and summer my father wore his Stetson hat and his Florsheim shoes. If he carried his coat folded over his arm the fold was inside out, the maker's label showing, testifying to where he had bought it and that in those days he had known better times.

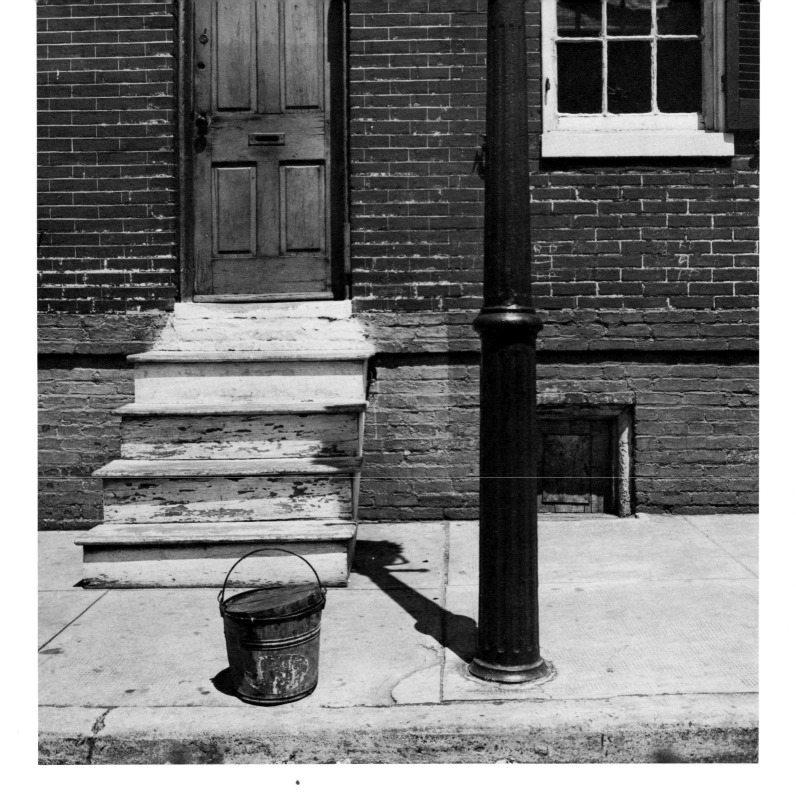

WHAT a man saw at night from the tower room in the freight yards, or remembered by day on a bench in the park, might have little to do with the place he claimed to be from. Chicago had an infinite variety of people; nevertheless there were people who proved to be missing. Otherwise, with so many to choose from, why dream them up? God's country had a great variety of places, and yet some places proved to be missing. Lone Tree, for example. It will not be found on the map. It is assembled from the real and imaginary pieces that a prodigal drags into exile with him, parts of a jigsaw he hopes to reassemble in a better place. He adds to these parts whatever seems to be missing, and as it slowly takes shape he begins to see it clearly. For the first time. It is a ghost town, and the exile is one of the ghosts. Lone Tree is born of this need for such a place, and once the place exists you can stock it with people. If inhabitants are wanted for an abandoned house, the house conjures them up. If a fly is missing between the cracked blind and the window, the scene conjures it up. Can a line be drawn between what is real and what is imaginary? When it comes time for me to salvage what I value, the larger part of what I value is what I have imagined, the smaller part is what I know to be gone, gone with the wind. From things about to disappear I turn away in time: I conjure them up.

GORDON BOYD needed a cemetery with lights where he could excavate the buried past.

"God's country?" he says. "It's lovely. Game, wildfowl and snotweed abound. Traveling from east to west one gets the impression of a verdant grassland, congenial to man, also the woolly mammoth and the dinosaur. Gone now. Spaghetti made in Omaha also popular in Italy. The State Capitol, finest in the nation, can be seen from a distance of thirty miles if there is no blowing dust. The people of the state, conservative by nature, living close to the soil and the round of seasons, are not swept by the tides of shifting opinion and still smilingly refer to Negroes as *coons*. Both live longer and go mad sooner. Mr. Charles Munger, celebrated gunman, is a native son. A restrained optimism characterizes the inlook and the outlook of these pioneer people who welcome the visitor with a 'Howdy, stranger!' and a friendly smile. Until a man proves himself bad he is considered good. Dust, as seen in *Life* magazine, continues to blow over the eastern states, and the state emblem, a stiffly pleated upper lip, symbolizes the spirit of its pioneer people in a new age."

ONE OF these pioneer people is Walter McKee: it is McKee's wife, Lois, who has the pleated upper lip. She might well be a fiction more important to Boyd than she is to McKee. She lacks McKee's restrained optimism and his affection for lost causes. McKee had once, to spare its suffering, tried to drown a poor bird that had flown into his windshield. He had thought it lifeless, but when its life was *threatened*, it had stiffened like a steel spring and hissed like a dragon. McKee had thought of Boyd. He had as little going for him as an injured bird but seemed as tough. From where did a battered, lifeless thing get so much strength? It had crossed McKee's mind that there was some subtle connection between that doomed creature, with its injured wing, and a high-flying dreamer whose wings had melted—like Boyd. When he put out his hand they both turned on him with their hate-filled eyes. One would think that McKee, who tried only to help, was their mortal enemy. The young hoodlums who gathered in the corner drugstores gave McKee such a look when he sidled past them, or when they drove up behind him and gave a loud blast on the horn. One of these boys, a kin of McKee, had run down and killed two of his own classmates, the way McKee's father would trap rabbits in the headlights and run them right into the ground.

Was it an accident that Lois McKee had Tom Scanlon for a father —a man who preferred to live in a dreamed-up time and an imaginary place? He passed his days in the deep blue freeze of the sky watching the wagon trains creak westward, crossing the plain like so many caterpillars with their fuzz burned off. Scanlon joined them: he sat on the buckboard whipping the oxen; he fought off packs of Indians; he burned in the deserts; he starved and froze in the mountains; on foot, through the clinkers of hell, he made his way to the gold fields of Paradise. Why not? He spent his Lone Tree winters with his feet in the oven, his ears, nose and wits frosted. It was no problem for him to return to a century he had never left. A fever compounded of ice-locked winters, kiln-fired summers, old Kansas City papers, pan-fried new potatoes, the boiled grounds of coffee and the last swipe of gravy, kept a man his wife and children thought better off dead more or less alive. Abandoned by his offspring, deserted by his wife, ignored by the polls, overlooked by the census, Tom Scanlon infected those who knew him with the virus of nostalgia, the cloudland stretched on the rack of his mind.

And Scanlon's wife? She went about her perpetual chores. The topless sky weighed on the plain like water, but it could not be said it kept her feet on the ground. A mindless wind moaned in the range, but it could not be said that she heard it. The lines of wash that criss-crossed the kitchen mercifully steamed the winter windows, the sleeves dripping like rain on the Omaha papers spread on the floor. In the summer the bed sheets flapped like sails on the strumming wires. First she fought to get them up, her teeth clenched on the clothespins, one of the wet sheets wrapped around her, the wire sagging to expose her chapped face to the wind. Then she fought to get them down, the children laughing to see their mother, like a headless chicken, groping toward the house with her wings flapping. In the winter, frozen stiff on the line, Scanlon's yellow underwear was like the husk of a man from which the living kernel had escaped, but the hard shell remained on her hands to be watered and fed. A lace of suds on her arms, her hips inclined on the drainboard, Scanlon's wife would stand with her hands in the dishpan, her unseeing eyes on the cracked green blind that shut off the view.

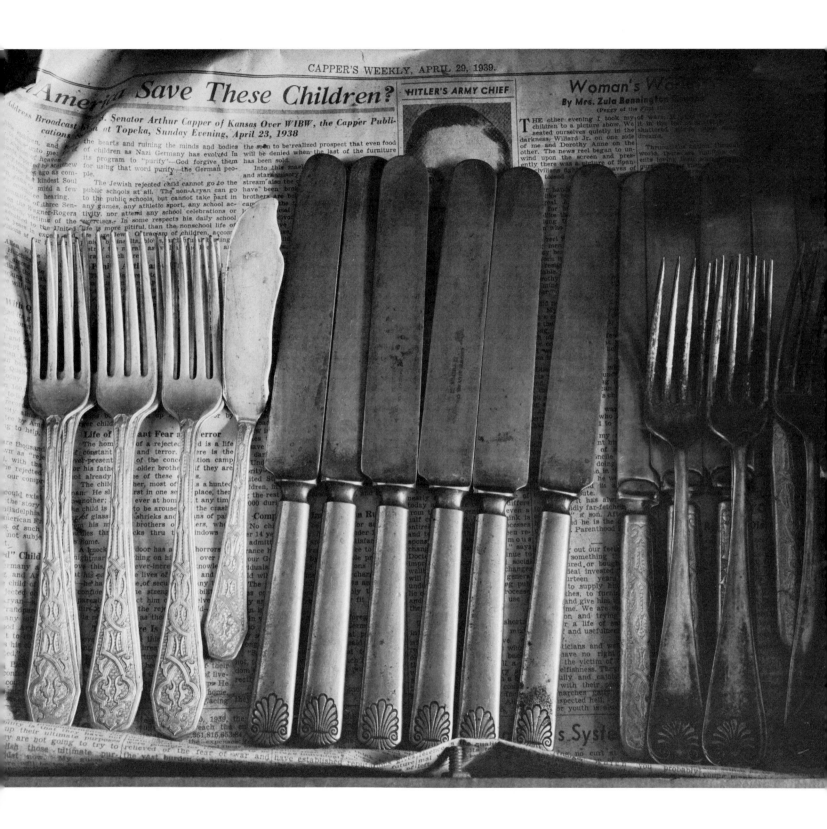

Tom Scanlon, according to his story, had been born in the rear of a Conestoga wagon, under a cottonwood tree once used as a stop by the pony express. This tree was said to loom on the plain like a mast, and the Indians buried their dead in its branches. He read it all somewhere. Or he got it from Cahow, Dr. Toomey or some other dreamer. He never saw a dead Indian, nor could he tell you what was meant by a Conestoga wagon. The one he claimed to have been born in (stored at the back of the stable, a cave for bats and small fry corn silk smoking parties) had come out from Omaha on a Burlington flatcar along with a balloon and William Jennings Bryan—part of a celebration to demonstrate that the century had turned. Perhaps the century did, but not Scanlon. At the moment the paving went to the east, he faced to the west. While forward-looking men were concerned with the future, he went about reassembling the past. He had to do it from scratch. There was little at hand in the way of spare parts. A lone tree, a hotel, a water tank, five or six trains daily that no longer stopped, a cattle loader like fragments of a battered pier swept by lapping waves of sand and tides of light. Not much, perhaps, but a beginning. More than enough for a piece of fiction. On the evidence the past was long dead and gone, but the script required that it be recovered, the fossil bones of Scanlon excavated at a site described as Lone Tree.

THAT'S HOW the lost good place became the great place to be from. Lone Tree is one, but God knows there are others: Soap Lake and Sunrise, Pisgah and Tecumseh, Serenity, Chloride, Fossil and Mystic. Some of these places prove to be real with people in them who answer their mail: some prove to be sur-real and answer only to God. Others, like Scanlon and Boyd, seem to be part of an expanding fiction; they answer only to the man who conjures them up. The landscape they inhabit is a windy ruin of ghosts. Something to do with the climate. Where the tongue is dry the mind is wet. Ghostly towns spring up when it rains, dry up when it stops. Bells clatter in empty belfries, shades stand immaterial at paneless windows, or bulge the screens of unhinged doorways, as if these places, known to be dead, had returned to life. But that's not uncommon. It's the buried past that comes to light. Where Scanlon's wife stands at the window a fly is trapped between the pane and the blind. She can see its shadow crawling. Perhaps she is waiting for it to buzz. The green blind, stitched with seams of light, sucks inward as a train roars past and the dangling cord leaves a chicken-like track in the dust on the sill. Lost on the wind, the moaning whistle is trapped in the range.

I<small>T's THE</small> nature of the place to generate such people as Scanlon, McKee and Lee Roy Momeyer. Lee Roy was a natural. He couldn't tell you how he did it himself. In three or four minutes, the motor idling, he could tune up a dual-carburetor system, but he didn't have the faintest idea how a carburetor *worked*. By ear he did it. All he got was a headache from the charts in the books. He liked to spend his time down in the grease pit, where he was not so tall he was always hitting something. To keep the grease out of his hair he wore caps made from the bottoms of paper bags. It gave him the look, one smart aleck said, of a Chinaman. There were all sorts of hot rods, but only Lee Roy had one with the chrome-plated mufflers up along the windshield, a little hot in the summer, but in the winter they melted the snow and ice. If he gunned it with the cutout open, it made you deef. All Lee Roy had to do when he needed an oil change was to tell some sap his own oil was dirty; he put nothing but the best drained oil into his own car. Down in the pit nobody pushed Lee Roy around, and when they made wisecracks he said, "Fuck the bastards!" He couldn't explain it. It just came natural to him and he played it by ear.

It's the custom of the country to go it alone, keep your own counsel, speak out in your sleep, play dead while awake, and hold fast to the faith that the good will prevail. It's the nature of the people to know right from left, good from bad, and a hawk from a handsaw. They brook no nonsense other than cold-blooded murder and a popular coach with more than three bad seasons. The shield of the country, sky-blue at the top, with fleur de Mazola in a scroll at the bottom, features a pleated upper lip on a field of shocked corn with golden sheaves of grain at the corners. There is little need for fiction since it persists as a way of life. The wells go deep, the buildings grow tall, the pillar of cloud on the horizon is screened for missiles, but the new land *Boom* derives from the widening quake in the sky. Out here the sky has always been the limit, and the land-locked plainsman was the first man to orbit. It's less a problem to get him up there than get him back down.

FROM an orbit that has never faltered my Aunt Winona sends me her love and the Lord's advice. My Uncle Dwight, a maverick sparkler in her sky of eternal stars, in ninety years has established a predictable orbit of his own. From the candied suburbs of the carrion City of Angels he writes his sister Winona a Christmas letter, still taunting her about articles of faith. His voice creaks. He walks with a cane. But in a firm clear hand he writes her that he plans to carry on till they carry him off. Since he'll be dead where he's going, little he cares how hot it is.

My FATHER, from his irregular orbit, wrote his son predictable letters, drilling his periods through the free stationery found in second-class hotel lobbies, the stub pointed pencil chained to the desk. *Dear Son—Have found you new mother.* Indicating he was lacking in neither faith nor talent. Most of his letters were written as want ads:

FATHER SEEKS MATRONLY WOMAN
FOR HOMELESS BOY.

He looked for and found himself in the Sunday Help Wanted column. His son, having in mind more readers, addresses himself *to whom it may concern.* He has spent most of his life speaking up for people who would rather remain silent (like his father) or live at peace with those who cry for help only in their sleep.

THE LAST time I saw my Uncle Dwight I asked him about my mother. It was known I had her eyes and her stubborn will. If she had lived, my life would have been different, no doubt about that. A pioneer woman, the first of the tribe to shoot at the moon. It had seemed to me strange, but was it so unusual? Moon-shooting has long been the custom of the country. Already we are thinking of remoter targets. The Grandfather began it, and I am still at it. Where do we go from here but into orbit? Where else but on the moon did my father spend most of his life?

THE LAST time I saw my father he was propped up in bed, the Sunday *Tribune* want ads spread on his lap. Men were wanted. He believed himself to be a wanted man. He proposed, once more, to find me a new mother and the best education the country afforded. He proposed to send me to Harvard, send me to Yale. For himself he asked no more than a chance to get back on his feet. That meant that his feet had to get back into the past. Day by day, week by week, this past got closer and his legs got longer. He had been a man of promise. He had been singled out as a man of caliber. T. P. Luckett, head of the U.P. commissary, instrumental in the spread of the Harvey system, had prophesied that my father would one day be president of the railroad. Which he might have been. As sure as God made little apples that is what he might have been if his wife and my mother had lived. He would have never lost his footing. I would not have lost my inheritance. According to my father, my Grandfather Osborn had lost millions of dollars in the Galveston flood, and once owned half the province of Saskatchewan. "Don't forget your father knows whereof he speaks," he would say, which was the manner of speech he reserved for the occasion. Saskatchewan is forever part of my lost inheritance.

On this occasion I asked him, point-blank, what my mother was like. He thought a moment, replied, "Wavy brown hair, blue eyes."

"I mean, what was she *like?*"

He was reminded that I was something like her, perhaps too much. He looked at me and said, "Kid, you got her eyes, you know that?" It is a custom of the country to know that. It is a custom of the people to look you in the eye, but not through it. To look you in the face, but not behind it. My father looked me in the eye and cried, "If your mother had lived, I wouldn't be lying here now!" He slapped the want ads in his lap until they buckled. He seldom expressed himself in such strong terms. Did he mean that my pioneer, sharpshooting mother would have kept him from jaywalking in Chicago? That her hand on his arm would have kept him firmly on his feet? Our lives would have been different, but it told me little of what she was like. Thirty years would pass before my father's ghost would put a similar question to his son. "Kid," he would say, "what was your father *really* like?" How can I tell, not knowing if he had his mother's eyes?

"Your mother was a remarkable woman," he said, closing the subject, "and don't you forget it." That is a custom of the country I still observe.

I HAVE not forgotten. She sees the new world through my eyes. Its topsoil can still be seen flowing under the bridges or breathed in the air of faraway places, and top men can be found who blow farther and wider than the soil. To get away from this place has been their passion, but few can report any measurable progress. Mine is on record. The landscape lies within me and proves to be a fiction that resists erosion. The child breathes it in the air and the orbiting astronaut will take it to the moon. Both landscapes generate the illusions common to the inhabitants of dry places, testifying to the notion that where men find the least there they see the most. Already those in orbit are learning to live out of this world. Already games are played where no rain falls and the grass is greener than the plastic carpets on the mounds of graves. Our feet in the dust bowl, our eyes on the Rose Bowl, we look for what is missing in the Lost & Found column, advertise for Help Wanted, or disappear without a trace to reappear in the snapshots of a dead man's wallet. The mother's eyes and hair provide clues for the recovery of what has never been lost.

From the freeway does this plain still roll like the sea or is it more like the floors of amusement parks? Are those blowouts on the rise or the sculptured bunkers of the leisure world's handicaps and its challenge? Will the child born this morning in De Kalb or Wahoo, Bauxite, Brimstone or Topeka look back in anger or wonder from a capsule in space or a tract on the moon? From that perspective the planet earth is a cosmic eye obscured by cataracts of cloud. The world concealed behind it is a science fiction, a metaphysical conceit. Is it a flaw in the planet or in the eye of the beholder that we prefer a far place to a near one, the earth a pad floating in space for the launching of dreams?

In the century since the Grandfather crossed the Missouri the land-scape has not perceptibly changed. To the north the smell of rain, to the south the smoke of dust, to the east rivers of earth still define God's country. On the daily commute we go into orbit, on the hour we take off. Is there more to come out of a higher standard of living than a predictably lower standard of feeling? Are we more moved by what little we know of the past than by what we dream about the future? Our talent is still for dreaming, and our recurrent dream is flight: a few hours away the luminous fueling stop of the moon. House or ark, sea or plain, shimmering mirages or figures of earth, God's country is still a fiction inhabited by people with a love for the facts.